Something Good Is Going To Happen To You

Choose the Imperishable, See the Invisible,
Do the Impossible

by

Oral Roberts

Albury Publishing
Tulsa, Oklahoma

Unless otherwise indicated, all Scripture quotations are taken from the *King James Version* of the Bible.

Something Good Is Going To Happen To You
Choose the Imperishable, See the Invisible,
Do the Impossible

ISBN 1-88008-928-9

Copyright © 1996 by Oral Roberts
Tulsa, Oklahoma 74171

Published by Albury Publishing
P.O. Box 470406
Tulsa, Oklahoma 74147

INTRODUCTION

The Bible says Moses was...**learned in all the wisdom of the Egyptians**...but that he chose **rather to suffer affliction with the people of God, than to enjoy the pleasures of sin**... (Acts 7:22; Hebrews 11:25). Moses chose God's riches over the riches of Egypt. When he did, he took the first step toward a miracle by choosing the imperishable of God.

When Moses took that step of obedience, he placed himself in position to see with the eye of faith. He chose the imperishable, which is the first step in God's Kingdom to seeing the invisible. Seeing the invisible gave him the courage he needed to do the impossible.

Doing the impossible is never easy. It's hard work! But once you choose the imperishable, then begin to see the invisible, suddenly you have the courage to do the impossible. Taking these three steps puts you in position to receive your miracle.

This book is intended to encourage you to take these three steps, and to remind you of what I've been telling you for fifty years—**Something Good Is Going To Happen To You!!!**

Oral Roberts

PART 1

CHOOSE THE IMPERISHABLE

Choosing rather to suffer affliction
with the people of God....
Hebrews 11:25

Before Moses could see the invisible, he was deeply involved in the lifestyle and culture of Pharaoh's court. He was ...**learned in all the wisdom of the Egyptians...** (Acts 7:22) to take Pharaoh's position while his own people, the Israelites, were under the cruelest bondage anyone could imagine.

But at the height of the suffering of his people, Moses remembered what his mother, Jochebed, had poured into her child's mind: "Moses, there is a God who is unlike the gods of the Egyptians or of any other people. He is not a visible God made of inanimate things without life or power. And someday, my son, you will develop the faith to see Him."

In time Moses came to a fork in his road. He had to trust the invisible enough to give him strength to take the next important step in life—choosing the imperishable. And it was at this fork in his road that he clearly saw suffering for God's cause as far greater than any visible benefit that could come to him as heir to Pharaoh's throne.

Moses had to admit there was "pleasure" in sin, but only "for a season." He had also come to know that like a puff of wind, such pleasure would be gone. So Moses separated himself and chose the imperishable.

Like Moses, anything and everything you choose to do to separate yourself from sin and to identify your life with God is literally imperishable. Neither you nor it will ever perish.

HUMBLE YOURSELF

Humble yourselves therefore under the mighty hand of God, that he may exalt you in due time.

1 Peter 5:6

Humility is a mysterious quality of God's imperishable life. When you think you have it, you don't.

It is said of Moses in Numbers 12:3 that he was ...**very meek, above all the men which were upon the face of the earth.** This was said of him following his humbling experience of forty years spent in the wilderness. Once he was walking the halls of Pharaoh's palace. Then, suddenly he was tending sheep.

The humble person is not aware he is humble. He neither belittles nor exalts himself. He accepts God's chosen place for him, whether it is in the forefront or the background. The words or actions of others do not debase, flatter, humiliate, honor, or in any other way affect a humble person. He retains his relationship with God, his Source, in every circumstance. His position among men is secondary.

And humility is not a permanent state. It is a goal we must constantly strive toward in order to avoid the pitfalls of pride. So the Scriptures repeatedly tell us to humble *ourselves.*

Another person may *try* to break our spirit, but we must initiate the process that leads to true humility. In Jesus' presence, we realize our nothingness and His *allness.* With this attitude, God can give you the miracle life you need. To go down is to go up in the imperishable.

PLANT A SEED OUT OF YOUR NEED

Whatsoever a man soweth,
that shall he also reap.
Galatians 6:7

Y ou don't plant seed unless you expect a harvest. Yet many dear Christians I know give out of a sense of duty—as if they "owe" God—and never expect a miracle. They say, "I give because I'm supposed to...so I don't expect anything back." But when Christians take this attitude they are violating the eternal law of God. Go back to Genesis. After God made the earth, He said;

While the earth remaineth, seedtime and harvest...shall not cease.

Genesis 8:22

In the New Testament, God said it like this:

...Whatsoever a man soweth, that shall he also reap.

Galatians 6:7

What these scriptures mean is, when you plant a seed, you are going to reap a harvest from that seed. What you give is a seed to plant. It is not a debt you owe. It is a seed you sow. If you need a smile, smile first. If you need love, give love. If you need healing, pray for someone else. This is a law of the imperishable.

Whatever you give—time, money, talent, friendship, concern, compassion—is a seed you plant. It *will* be multiplied. This is the law of increase. A seed planted reproduces itself. It will increase and bear fruit.

DON'T LET GO!

And having done all, to stand.
Ephesians 6:13

For most people, Friday is the end of a work-week when they can walk away to the weekend and enjoy some rest and recreation. Faith, however, doesn't have any week-ends. You just can't take a break and forget about it for a while.

Miracles must be made to happen just like your workweek is made to happen—by you!

God isn't going to have Jesus die and rise from the dead again. He isn't going to put any more miracle power in your world. God, the full God, is here. So once you use your faith in the imperishable to start a miracle, you must stand firm in your faith.

And don't interrupt your faith. If you relax your stance, the miracle you started will not be completed. You have just shut God's channel to get it to you.

I know, I've been there time and time again. And still I have to remind myself: Oral, stay in faith; Oral, keep believing God; Oral, never give in; keep choosing the imperishable; Oral, never interrupt your faith!

HEAR HIS WORDS

This is my beloved Son: hear him.
Mark 9:7

I f there is a doubt in your mind that God speaks to you, or that you can hear Him, look at Mark 1:11. Those who witnessed John the Baptist baptizing Jesus in the river Jordan heard the Father say:

This is my beloved Son: hear him.

God was speaking. They heard His words. They understood that God speaks. He speaks to people, to every person.

Jesus went about talking to people and they "heard" His words. On one occasion He said, **Let these sayings sink down into your ears** (Luke 9:44). In other words Jesus said, be listening so intently that you actually hear what I'm saying and it becomes a part of you. When you do, you will know the way of God and the power of God in your life. Choose to hear My words. They are imperishable.

Listen to the sayings of King David:

...Today if ye will hear his voice,

Harden not your heart, as in the provocation, and as in the day of temptation in the wilderness.

Psalm 95:7-8

Be ready to hear God. Then be open to His words.

THERE IS A DEVIL

*Greater is he that is in you,
than he that is in the world.*
1 John 4:4

You may not like what I'm going to say to you now. It's your choice. But I must say it, or I will fail God. I will fail you. I will fail myself.

There is a devil. He is real. And if you deny that the devil exists, you have to deny God, the Bible, and all of human experience. You have to say everything happens by chance. When something goes wrong you have to say, "I'm just unlucky. The odds are against me." Or, "Life is just not worth living."

If you say and believe any one of those things, you are really in trouble. You've got to get hold of yourself and declare: "I am going back to the God who created me. The God who sent His Son to die for me on Calvary to rise from the dead to give me life and give it more abundantly. I am going to set myself in agreement with God to bring me out of this mess and make me a whole person, in spite of everything the devil has been trying to do to me."

Next, you're going to have to take a step of faith above and beyond every doubt you have ever had. A step that takes you above every negative feeling you have ever given birth to. And above every lie about God you have ever entertained. You are going to have to make the commitment to believe that God is a million, billion, trillion times greater than the devil, and that He loves you with a love that surrounds you. He is closer to you now than even your breath. And He is right now *sending miracles toward you!*

There are two powers in life, not three or four or more—just two: God and the devil. This is a truth of the imperishable.

DON'T BLAME GOD

Your adversary the devil, as a roaring lion, walketh about, seeking whom he may devour.
1 Peter 5:8

The devil is the one who is hurling every bad thing possible against you. So don't accuse God of doing it or blame Him as if He did.

Jesus knew the devil had once been the archangel, Lucifer, the highest and greatest of all the archangels. The devil was the one closest to God's throne, the one who was actually the hovering presence over the Father. Lucifer was the son of the morning, God's most trusted angel. Therefore, he was given the greatest powers and responsibilities. But he allowed envy and covetousness to enter his spirit, and he turned against God. Lucifer attempted to be above God, to take His place and become what God alone is: King of the universe (Ezekiel 28, Isaiah 14:12, and Luke 10:18).

Jesus was there when Satan was thrown out of heaven. He saw it all happen and was part of the triune God who placed the devil as the prince of the power of the air (Ephesians 2:2), and the god of this world (2 Corinthians 4:4). And Jesus was there when Satan was reduced to the one who became: as a roaring lion.

Lucifer is not the Prince of Peace. Only Jesus Christ of Nazareth is the Prince of Peace. Neither is Lucifer the King and the God of the universe. Only the eternal Father is the King and God of the universe. The Bible says Lucifer is not even a lion. He is "as" a roaring lion. The devil can roar, but he has no real power except what man chooses to give him.

Jesus knew all this about the devil and more. So when bad came against Him, He called the devil what he was: a liar (John 8:44), killer, thief, destroyer (John 10:10), and deceiver (Revelation 20:10). Those who choose the imperishable know all of this to be true. They can deal with the devil like Jesus, instead of being fooled.

POURED OUT BLESSINGS

And pour you out a blessing, that there shall not be room enough to receive it.
Malachi 3:10

Those who choose God's imperishable can expect a blessing back from Him that will be much bigger than anything they thought it would be.

Hear that carefully. God has a greater blessing for you than you have imagined. He says that the windows of heaven will be opened to you and that He will pour out a blessing that you will not be able to contain! In Luke 6:38 we read about this type of blessing in similar words, **pressed down, and shaken together, and running over.** God has an abundance for you in all areas of your life.

What's the greatest miracle that you can imagine receiving from God today?

Well, think again, because the blessing God has in mind for you is even greater!

MORE THAN ONE WAY

*He anointed the eyes of
the blind man with the clay.*
John 9:6

God uses many methods to bring His healing power to those who are seeking the imperishable. One of His methods is prayer.

God encourages us to **lay hands on the sick...and pray one for another** for healing. (See Mark 16:18, James 5:16.) I know this method works.

I've laid my hands on more than a million people during my lifetime, praying and with faith believing for mighty miracles. I've seen the lame walk. I've watched as the blind begin to see. I've seen the deaf hear. I've watched goiters, tumors, all sorts of abnormal growths disappear before my eyes. Yes, God heals through the method of prayer—and nobody could ever convince me otherwise.

Another wonderful method of personal prayer through which God heals is Holy Communion.

And God heals through medicine. He has allowed men and women of science to discover the healing chemicals He placed in the earth, to learn how to use them to help us get well. He has allowed physicians to develop great skills in surgery and in therapy to restore us to wholeness.

God also works through a balanced diet, the loving words and concern of others, and through climate.

God has unlimited resources for healing us. But it's up to us to not limit God or put a stop to His many miracle methods that He wants to bring into our lives.

DETERMINATION
AND DESIRE

He shall give thee the desires of thine heart.
Psalm 37:4

Do you have a heart's desire? If you do, then you have a determination to see it happen in your life. It's not just a whim, or a wish, it's a deep, motivating force that you think about day in and day out.

The Bible has many stories of people who were determined to get their miracle who obeyed God, believed His Word, and received what they desired!

Abraham was determined. When God asked him to sacrifice his son Isaac, Abraham determined in his heart that he would obey God and trust the consequences to Him. Although he loved his son more than he loved anything on the face of the earth, Abraham's highest desire was to love and obey God.

When Abraham operated out of that desire in preparing to sacrifice his son, God saw that his desire was pure and Isaac was spared. God provided a ram to be sacrificed in Isaac's place. Abraham had chosen the imperishable. Hebrews 11:10 said he was looking for...**a city which hath foundations, whose builder and maker is God.**

Are you, like Abraham, determined today to seek God's highest will for your life? To obey Him fully? To believe God's Word?

Noah was also determined. He kept building the ark even when everyone criticized him. He could have easily doubted God. No one had ever heard of rain, or even thought about a flood that might destroy the earth.

But Noah obeyed God and remained steady. He kept building the ark for more than a hundred years, though he could have easily given up. But he had chosen the imperishable. Hebrews 11:7 says that Noah was ...**warned of God of things not seen as yet....**

Are you willing, like Noah, to ignore the criticism of others? Are you willing to stay steady in your faith no matter what the opposition might be, or how long your miracle might take?

Like Abraham and Noah, be determined to trust God. He will bring your miracle to pass!

PART 2

SEE THE INVISIBLE

For he endured, as seeing him who is invisible.
Hebrews 11:27

As I pointed out in Part I, when Moses was rescued out of slavery by the princess of Egypt to be raised as the prince of Egypt, he eventually came to a crossroads. It was there that he made the decision to honor and to see, through faith, the invisible God.

"He is not a visible God made of inanimate things without life or power," were the words of his mother, Jochebed. "His name is Jehovah," she continued, "He is invisible. And someday, my son, you will develop the faith to see our invisible God. Not by your natural eyes, but by your spirit. This is the one God, the only God, who will deliver us. Your faith, Moses, will see beyond the visible barriers that cloud the vision of all people without faith. And there will surely be a moment of destiny for you and for all of mankind. Moses, you will see the invisible so that the ways of the invisible God are made more real than anything in this world, and the light will shine upon every man."

If you have reached the point in your life where visible things can only do so much for you and you are feeling limited to the point of frustration, if you are heading toward utter hopelessness—I want to tell you that there is a way for you. You can take the limits off God by believing inside of yourself that there is a God. He may be invisible— but He is more real and alive than the breath in your nostrils!

EXPECT A MIRACLE

According to your faith be it unto you.
Matthew 9:29

Expect the invisible to become visible. Miracles are passing your way. Expect them. They are coming toward you and past you every day. When you plant seeds and pray in faith, you can rejoice. You can believe that God is healing you *now*—today! Look for miracles to happen and thank God for every one, large or small. When your heart is expectant, then you can recognize and receive God's miracles every day.

As I have said, and I believe, the secret of abundant life is in expecting miracles from our risen Lord.

I believe that God is working many divine healings this very day. I believe there is great gladness of heart as God pours out His Holy Spirit upon His people.

GOD IS YOUR SOURCE

*But my God shall supply all
your need according to his riches
in glory by Christ Jesus.
Philippians 4:19*

My God.... The Bible says *my God* shall supply all your needs. It doesn't say that the U.S. Government will do it. It doesn't say that your boss, your job, or your business will do it. It says *my God* will do it. So if someone lets you down, it doesn't really matter, *because God never lets you down.*

God often uses man as the means, but God Himself is the source. Man is only an instrument of the source.

...**shall supply**.... Jesus looks on a need in the most positive way. To Him, a need exists to be met. This is what God's Word says: "God *shall supply* all your need." *Shall* is a very strong word. It is emphatic! In other words, the moment your need faces you, God's *shall supply* promise goes into effect.

Your needs, no matter what they are, are a legitimate claim upon God's limitless resources. God is more than willing and able to supply the Christian's needs in full! You give God your best, as He says in Luke 6:38, then ask Him for His best. And when you ask from a sincere heart, God moves.

...*all* your need.... Jesus does not fragment your life into different parts. He is concerned with *all your needs*. No need should intimidate or bully you. Whatever your need is—Jesus came to meet that need! It is included in "*all* your need."

...**according to his riches**.... God controls all sources of supply. If one source is wiped out, God will supply from another if you look to Him.

Your need can *appear* to exceed God's abundance. However, His supply is according to *His* riches! And *His* riches are *always* more than equal to your need!

...**in glory by Christ Jesus.** God didn't say He would supply your needs *with* His riches in heaven, but *according to* His riches in heaven *by Christ Jesus.* That means here, *in the now.* God is telling you that all you need is already on deposit in heaven, in His realm of the invisible, payable in earthly currency, through Christ. He is the Source of your complete supply. Every need you will ever have has been provided for by His glorious riches. Faith to see the invisible, brings them into the visible.

MIRACLES EVERY DAY

Ask, and it shall be given you;
seek, and ye shall find; knock,
and it shall be opened unto you.
Luke 11:9

The finders in Luke 11:9 are the seekers of God's invisible realm. The door openers are those who knock, and the receivers are those who *expect* when they ask.

When you walk with Jesus every day in Seed-Faith living, God will send you miracles every day. But you must expect them so that you recognize them when they come. Otherwise, miracles may just pass you by. Seed-Faith sees into and expects from God's realm of the invisible.

Miracles are coming to you or passing by you every day. If you are really expecting them, they are yours.

Every day you can expect miracles in...

> your physical body
> your mind
> your spiritual life

      your finances

      your relationships.

So be expecting as an asker as you ask God for His blessing every day. Be expecting as a seeker as you search into God's invisible realm. Then get ready to be a receiver as the doors you knock on begin opening and the blessings of God's invisible realm start overtaking you.

SOMETHING GOOD
IS GOING TO HAPPEN
TO YOU!

The goodness of God endureth continually.
Psalm 52:1

Why do I say something good is going to happen to you, even when sometimes things look dark? Because God loves you. There are so many good things God *wants* to give you. If you look to Him as your Source and give Him all that you are and all that you do, He will bring great things to pass in your life. This is Seed-Faith living at its best! Practice it consistently—every day, every hour, every minute!

Your miracle begins when you stop being negative and start being positive. Being positive is trusting, planting, and receiving! Being negative is doubting. When you doubt, you are planting bad seed. You are robbing yourself of miracles.

You can face life with optimism and enthusiasm when you are aware that God is alive! He is only invisible to those who choose not to see Him through faith.

SOMETHING GOOD

God is good! God is near! Completely believe and fully expect that something good will happen to you today...and it will!

EXPECT THE UNEXPECTED

Now unto him that is able to do exceeding abundantly above all that we ask or think.
Ephesians 3:20

Many years ago while conducting a crusade in Seattle, I met a seventy-year-old man by the name of William Skrinde. He was an inventor, and one of the things he had invented was a part for the wheel of a Jeep. But he had been unable to sell it. He had literally poured out his life and finances in trying to prove the part's value, but Jeep wasn't interested.

By the time Mr. Skrinde came to our crusade, he and his wife were living hand-to-mouth. In addition to their meager Social Security checks, he was working in a convalescent home, making about $200 a month.

However, during the crusade, Mr. Skrinde and his wife accepted Jesus and soon thereafter accepted the Seed-Faith principles of the Bible. It was a new idea to him, but when he seized it he found himself opening up to God's help in a way he hadn't thought possible.

During one of the meetings Mr. Skrinde attended, the Lord led me to say, "Look for God to give you ideas. In fact, there may be something God already has for you that you haven't seen. Look around! Open your eyes. See what God has given you. Be expectant, even from unexpected sources."

After that meeting, Mr. Skrinde went home, climbed up into his attic and found the papers he had drawn up years before. He felt led in his spirit to try one more time with the makers of the Jeep.

And this time Jeep bought the invention! As a result, Mr. Skrinde became very wealthy.

When I first met Mr. Skrinde, he was stooped over—not only physically, but emotionally, mentally, and spiritually. But as he gradually got more and more into the rhythm of planting his seeds of faith while expecting God to open His sources of supply, he began to straighten up.

Eventually, Mr. Skrinde became one of the largest contributors to Oral Roberts University. When I walk across the ORU campus, I see his imprint on building after building, including the great pipe organ in Christ's Chapel. He expected the unexpected. And today it's almost impossible for me to remember that stoop-shouldered, worn-out man with his lost dreams and meager income.

WHAT IS FAITH?

*Now faith is the substance of things
hoped for, the evidence of things not seen.
Hebrews 11:1*

What is faith? Faith is seeing the visible things around you and believing that behind every one of them is the invisible God who made them all. Faith is allowing yourself to feel again that deep feeling you first felt as a little child that told you there is Someone out there beyond your physical sight...at the edge of your fingertips.

Faith is taking hold of your will to determine that you believe in this God, and that He is all-powerful, all-wise, and everywhere present at the same time. Faith is believing that God is a good God and that He who created you sent you a Savior, Jesus Christ of Nazareth.

Faith is yielding your spirit to its built-in urge to allow the Holy Spirit to supernaturally empty you of doubt. Doubt of God's existence, doubt of His goodness, or doubt of God's care is removed from the life of one who has faith. In its place God gives confidence that you know that you know God is real—and He is your God!

It is in this generation—yours and mine—that we by faith see beyond all limitations of spirit, mind, body, and circumstances. Your faith's sight of God goes beyond 20/20 vision. You see things in perspective. But to see the invisible you have to reach down into your real inner self on the inside of your body called your spirit—and choose to see. The evidence for you to see the invisible is everywhere. Work with your faith, let it soar within you to see beyond all things visible to Him who is invisible. He is the only reality you will ever know.

LISTENING

My sheep hear my voice...
John 10:27

Recently, a noted heart doctor walked up to me on the golf course. "Oral," he said, "will you write a little book on how a person can hear God's voice? How I can really hear Him in my spirit?"

I told him, "You'll be surprised just how simple it is to hear God speak inside of you. In fact, you have to become child-like in your thinking and just listen!"

He said, "You mean if I listen I will hear God speak to me?"

I said, "Yes. Try it. You'll hear God because He speaks to every-one."

Again, it takes commitment to listen. God is invisible, and He speaks to our hearts.

I've been five decades in this ministry, and the older I get, the simpler I believe it is. But if I had it to do over again, I'd listen more.

I know I would have heard God more often, and more clearly, if I had realized how simple it is.

However, I praise Him that I *have* listened to His voice. Because of it, He brought me out of nothing and made my life worth something. So for the rest of my life I'm absolutely committed to listen, listen, listen.

I CAN FEEL HIM TUGGING ON THE LINE

But when the Comforter is come...even the Spirit of truth...he shall testify of me.
John 15:26

I f you could see into the invisible world of the Spirit, you would see a line connecting you directly with God. That line is the Holy Spirit. He connects you with God the Father so you can make daily contact with Him, telling Him exactly what you need.

From God's end of the *line*, He can see you clearly. His love and care for you are greater than any you've ever known. And His words of life are coming across the *line*. So if you are in connection, *and* if you are listening, you can hear Him in terms that you understand right at the point of your need.

This understanding of our line to God is like the little boy who was flying a kite. He kept letting out the kite string until after a while it literally soared so high it was out of sight.

Then a man walking by saw the little boy standing with his hands stretched out holding onto what looked like a string. The little boy was looking up, but there was nothing in sight. So the man asked, "Sonny, what are you doing?"

"Flying a kite," the boy said.

"Flying a kite? I don't see any kite," the man answered back.

"All the same, it's up there," the boy said.

"Well, I can't see it," the man said again.

"Still, it's up there," the boy said.

Finally, the man asked, "Well, if you can't see it, how do you know it's up there?"

So finally, the boy said, "Mister, I can feel it tugging on the line."

This story describes so well how you and I can know God is up there through feeling Him speak to our inner being down here. He tugs on our connecting line by speaking through an impression inside of us that is different from any human expression. The impression will always draw us toward God and point us in the right direction for our lives. The one tugging at us with the impression is the Comforter, the Holy Spirit, who Jesus sent to connect us with God the Father.

THE QUESTION OF *WHY*

So then faith cometh by hearing....
Romans 10:17

Faith to see God's invisible comes to you in many ways. But the most powerful, the most sure, the most effective way is by the Word of God. As you read and study it with an open mind and a hungry heart, and as you hear it preached and taught as God is **confirming the word with signs following** (Mark 16:20), your faith grows.

But you may ask, "Oral, how does all of this help me with my why questions?"

I'll tell you how it helps. It takes you to your *Source*: *God*!

Still you may ask, "But will looking to God as my Source and only to Him answer all my whys?"

My answer to this question is: YES! Some of your whys will be answered instantly and dramatically through prayer and Bible study. Others will be answered over a period of time. Still others will be answered by a miracle of God so that the why will be gone forever.

And faith will give you a hope of heaven. In heaven all your whys will be answered for the simple reason that when God raises you from the dead in the resurrection—there will be no more whys. Why? Because there will be no more devil to have to face! You will be with God forever!

If you have whys, your answers are in God's Word.

GOD IS YOUR REWARDER

He is a rewarder of them
that diligently seek him.
Hebrews 11:6

F or years—in fact, during all of my growing-up years—I never dreamed that God was a rewarder.

I grew up under the kind of teaching that said if we stepped aside the wrong way, we would be slapped down by God or even cast into hell. So I got all mixed up in my thinking, and I went for years with the wrong idea about our invisible God.

I'm still learning the truth about God. But had I known while growing up that He is a *rewarder*, I think I would have dreamed a different dream when I was a teenager. I never would have run away from my mother and father and plunged into a life of sin.

WHAT ARE GOD'S REWARDS?

If you think that God rewards you with sickness in your body, you are wrong. And if you think that He rewards you with poverty, depression, loneliness, or a long-faced religion that robs you of joy, you are wrong!

God rewards you with a relationship with Him that puts joy in your soul, a shine on your face, a sparkle in your eyes, a lift to your shoulders, and a spring in your step. He rewards you with blessings, health, prosperity, love, purpose, fulfillment, and meaning.

God is a rewarder, and His rewards are good!

IT IS GOD'S WILL TO HEAL

I am the Lord that healeth thee.
Exodus 15:26

A Roman centurion came to Jesus one day seeking healing for his servant. He told Jesus about how his servant was in bed paralyzed and in great agony. After hearing the centurion's words, Jesus did not hesitate for a moment. Immediately He said:

...I will come and heal him.

Matthew 8:7

In that one statement of absolute fact, Jesus was establishing something for you and me today, and for every human being who has ever lived:

IT IS GOD'S WILL FOR YOU TO BE WELL.

Never again believe that God wants you to be sick. That is a lie of the devil. God's desire is for you to be healed. It is His will that you be whole in spirit, mind, and body; and that you be prosperous in your finances, and in your relationships.

God is not only your source, your rewarder, and the rebuker of the devourer in your life—He is your healer. He is still going about doing good and healing all who are oppressed of the devil (Acts 10:38), but you must seek Him as the centurian, to realize God's will.

PART 3

DO THE IMPOSSIBLE

With God nothing shall be impossible.
Luke 1:37

The first step in doing the impossible is putting your faith in God. Now consider Moses doing the impossible. When he first heard God speaking in his spirit, he literally obeyed, trying each time to put God's way and God's plan above his own. That took commitment.

One thing I want to point out that is very important is that Moses did those things through struggle. Moses struggled to stop playing around with sin. He struggled to leave his life of glory and prestige that awaited him in Pharaoh's court. And he struggled to get down in the trenches with the children of Israel who were suffering under Pharaoh's whip.

Moses found no easy way, no shortcut, no free lunch—just plain struggle. But if he hadn't used his faith to see the invisible God so he could choose the imperishable, he would never have done the impossible.

I tell you on the authority of the infallible Word of God, and out of the experience of every believer who has accomplished anything, including my own life, you do the impossible through struggle.

I am honored that God has allowed me to travel this far through faith and struggle and have seen Him enable me to do the impossible. I exalt Him in it.

And I don't like the struggle or persecution or any of the stuff Satan and men throw at me constantly. But they always overplay their hand, particularly when I choose to reach down inside myself and declare that I will obey God, and that I won't quit, and that I won't be defeated. What they have tried to make impossible, God has made possible.

Only you can hold God back from blessing you. He created you with the inner ability to *choose the imperishable*, to *see the invisible*, to *do the impossible.* Just like getting in your car, turning the ignition key, and shifting into drive, you can turn your faith loose this very instant to do the impossible, with God.

So don't refuse the struggle. God will help you through. Make up your mind to start doing it *now!*

FORGIVENESS

Pray one for another,
that ye may be healed.
James 5:16

To do the impossible, you must constantly be planting seeds of forgiveness. When we walk in forgiveness, God is unhindered in blessing our lives.

An unforgiving attitude resists God's presence. It is poisonous. It brings sickness and keeps us from being healed. So God tells us to pray for the person whom we feel has wronged us that we might be healed in our own body, mind, and spirit.

With your prayer you are planting a seed of love and obedience that God can multiply back to you over and over again. The seed of forgiveness is one of the most powerful seeds you will ever plant because it will keep you in God's peace and keep you close to Him.

NEUTRALIZE CRITICISM WITH FORGIVENESS.

Vengeance is mine; I will repay, saith the Lord.
Romans 12:19

The fear of criticism is one of the worst fears we can allow ourselves to develop. And if you want to do the impossible with God, you will have your critics. What people say about us is important. But it is wrong to let their opinion of us determine our happiness.

So a good policy to follow when you are criticized is to ask yourself if it is true. Then if it is, have the courage to change. And if it is not, take the criticism, put it in the hands of God, and leave it there.

But most important is to neutralize your critic's words by forgiving him. When you do, you are planting a powerful seed for a great miracle in your own life.

Forgive him whether he asks you to or not. This is what Jesus did. ...**Father, forgive them**, He said while hanging on the cross, **for they know not what they do** (Luke 23:34).

Use the power of prayer when seeking to do God's will. Put your critic in the hands of God. Forgive him. He will deal with him more effectively than you can. Instead of striking back, have the good grace to let God be the paymaster. Then go on about the important business of living, planting seed, and expecting miracles. God will take care of your critics. Your forgiving attitude will disarm the worst of enemies and bring a miracle your way.

CONFESS YOUR FEAR

*For the thing which I greatly feared
is come upon me, and that which
I was afraid of is come unto me.*
Job 3:25

To do the impossible you must handle your fears. While viewing the collapse of everything dear to him, Job said, ...**The thing which I greatly feared is come upon me**... (Job 3:25). He put into words what he had actually done to himself and admitted, "I feared...I was afraid."

It is good to admit your fear. Get it out of your system. So confess it to God. Plant it as a seed and expect God, the Source of supply, to bring the best your way.

Job had believed the worst. He believed terrible things were going to happen—and they did. This is what constitutes fear, believing the lies of the enemy instead of believing God, who is your source of total supply.

Believing in God's goodness and knowing that He will send good things your way is believing in the truth. And the truth He has always wanted us to know is, "Something good is going to happen to you." When you have this attitude, it puts you in the right position for the blessings of God to come to you and remain with you.

IT MAY BE CLOSER
THAN YOU THINK

*Now he that ministereth seed to the
sower both minister bread for your food,
and multiply your seed sown....*
2 Corinthians 9:10

I f you just think about it, you've probably already sown many seeds of faith. But you haven't been expecting from the only real source of total supply—God. So what should you look for?

An idea.

An opportunity.

A relationship.

It may be something you've inherited, something you bought long ago and forgot. Or something you started and just haven't finished. It may be special favor with someone, a vacant lot, an empty building, an unused room, a piece of equipment, or something you've given up on and put away.

Your miracle may be closer than you think. Look around! Be observant! Be expectant!

Remember that Jesus used two fishes and a few loaves to work a miracle that fed five thousand people when a little boy gave what he had.

Another time He asked a fisherman for the loan of his fishing boat to preach from. Then when He was finished, He shocked the man by telling him there was a net-breaking, boat-sinking load of fish right there in the same waters where they had failed to catch anything.

God is all around you like the air you breathe. He is under you like the ground you walk on. And He is above you like clouds in the sky. He is the source of all good.

Reach down into your innermost being, and by an act of your will, open yourself up to God's next great idea, His next great miracle, and do the impossible. Act on it now!

REMEMBER YOUR MIRACLE

Lay hands on the sick, and they shall recover.
Mark 16:18

When God blesses us with a healing miracle, we must never forget to honor Him by going forward with His plan. Shortly after my healing from tuberculosis began at age seventeen, I realized that my excitement was dying down and that the surge of new health in my lungs appeared to be waning. Doubt began to harass me, and I felt weaker and weaker.

Then I learned one of the greatest lessons of my life. My mother discovered me one afternoon sitting with my back to the wall on the side of the house and she said, "Oral, you're beginning to believe you weren't really healed, aren't you?"

"Well, Mamma," I replied, "why do I still feel so weak? Why don't I feel strong like I did the other night when I was prayed for?"

Then Mamma said this, "Oral, don't forget you've been sick a long time. You've been five months in bed and lost the power to walk. The tuberculosis had taken root in your lungs before that. God has begun to heal you and your miracle has started."

"So when you feel weak, think back to the power of God you felt surging through your body, opening your lungs to breathe free again, and remember that was God's touch, His instant touch of healing in you. But it may take weeks, or maybe months, for the miracle of complete healing to happen."

Mamma was right, and I did exactly what she said. With every discouragement—and there were lots of them—I remembered the night God's healing power entered my body and opened up my lungs. I was able to breathe all the way down without hemorrhaging. So I relived it in my spirit and mind over and over.

Then slowly, but surely, I felt my strength being renewed. Within twelve months I was restored from a skeleton-like 120 pounds to a robust 165 pounds.

There was a flash in my eyes, a lift in my shoulders, a spring in my step, and faith in my soul.

Time after time I have looked back and tried to understand the wisdom my mother gave me. I believe she was telling me not to interrupt my faith, not to stop the making of that miracle to restore my life—and keep it restored.

HOLD ON TO THE END

And if there be any praise,
think on these things.
Philippians 4:8

I f you need a miracle to start doing the impossible, faith can bring it. However, letting up on your faith can retard that same miracle, or stop it altogether. So when anything strikes at my health today, I get serious about it instantly. I have developed an attitude, a lifestyle, a habit, with the way I use my faith. I can't say it's perfect, but it beats any other way I know.

First, I start getting hold of myself. I shift the gears of my mind to think on the great things God has done for me—like that first burst of healing energy in my tubercular lungs.

It's amazing how many miracles God has done in you that you can't explain in rational terms. But you *can* purposefully bring them to mind, and you can literally *think on them*.

I often turn to Philippians 4:8 and read it over and over.

SOMETHING GOOD

Finally, brethren, whatsoever things are true, whatsoever things are honest, whatsoever things are just, whatsoever things are pure, whatsoever things are lovely, whatsoever things are of good report; if there be any virtue, and if there be any praise, think on these things.

It is the devil's business to tempt you to forget God and His providence in your life and to have you think only on the bad things. But **greater is he that is in you, than he that is in the world** (1 John 4:4), and here God strongly tells you to think on whatever is:

> true...
> honest...
> just...
> pure...
> lovely...

of good report...
virtuous...
praiseworthy....

And He wants us to think this way both in our past and in our *now*.

The good thing is, we have the God-given power to think like this, because to do the impossible we must think like this. I know when I do it, I am enormously strengthened in every way.

ACTIVATE YOUR MIRACLE

Bring ye all the tithes into the storehouse...
Malachi 3:10

To live in God's miracle flow, He says that there is something we must do to activate His flow toward us. It's like putting a key into a locked door. He says, **Bring ye all the tithes into the storehouse.**

But you may ask, "Why does God need my money?" So I will answer, He doesn't need it for His sake. He has all the gold and the silver of the entire earth.

The earth is the Lord's, and the fulness thereof....

Psalm 24:1

God wants you to give for *your* sake. He says your giving is for two reasons. First, you give that His work might go on in the entire earth. So that missions teams might reach into the darkest nations with God's healing power. So television programs might span the nation with the message that "God is a good God." So churches might be planted and souls might be saved. So people might be delivered. So prayer and medicine might be combined. So people might see the Word of God come alive before their eyes.

God wants His work to go on here on earth with churches that are full and alive with miracles, signs, and wonders, so that heaven will be populated.

Second, God says your giving is going to trigger a response from Him. He is going to prove Himself to you by pouring out a blessing on you.

I don't know how you feel about it, but this excites me. I want to see God's work multiplied on this earth until every person has heard the Gospel and has been touched by God's power! And I want God's blessing pouring back into my own life so I can bless other people again! That's the two-fold response that I want in my life! What about you?

WALK INTO VICTORY!

And I will rebuke
the devourer for your sakes...
Malachi 3:11

God wants to rebuke the devourer—the devil himself—who is trying to destroy your life. It is the devil's purpose to hinder your faith and to keep you locked out of God's imperishable, invisible plans.

Psalm 106:9 says God **rebuked the Red sea** and it dried up so the children of Israel could walk through on dry land. Today, God wants to rebuke the trouble that is blocking your way, so you can also walk through to victory!

Are problems threatening to overwhelm you? Are you feeling like things are out of control? Jesus wants to rebuke the forces that are coming against you today!

In Matthew 8:26, Jesus **rebuked the wind and the sea** and calmed the waves threatening to swamp the disciples' boat.

SOMETHING GOOD

In Luke 4:39 Jesus **rebuked the fever** from Peter's mother-in-law and she rose up out of the sickness. Jesus wants to rebuke the trouble that has you down so that you can walk in victory!

You are not alone in this life of the invisible. If you are a tither, God's power is rebuking the devourer. His Spirit is working for you.

PUSHING YOUR WAY THROUGH TO JESUS

If I may touch but his clothes,
I shall be whole.
Mark 5:28

T he woman with the issue of blood was determined to receive from God. She pushed her way through the crowd until she could touch the hem of Jesus' garment herself. And she received the healing that no one, no medicine or treatment had been able to provide for her during twelve long years of illness.

If you have somehow been enduring a similar situation in your life, it is time to press into God to receive your healing. It is time for you to make the decision to choose the imperishable way of God's kingdom so you can see His invisible realm. It is time to believe that God is a good God. And it is time to do the impossible in the strength of believing faith.

But are you willing to go after your miracle with all of your strength?

God has put determination—a deep desire for miracles—in each one of us. No matter what it takes, no matter what anyone may think, no matter what anybody may say, no matter what criticism we receive, we can be determined to stand strong and to believe the facts:

Jesus wants to bless you with imperishable, eternal life!

Jesus wants to use you in the power of His invisible realm!

Jesus wants to prosper you as you give Him your entire life!

And Jesus wants to heal you.

In His timing.

In His method.

It is God's will for you to be whole—spirit, mind, and body. Trust Him to be your Savior today! Start planting new seeds of faith. Read God's Word, and do what He says. Put away all fearful thinking and let God's plan of blessing come into your life.

Like Moses, you too have a destiny to choose the imperishable, see the invisible, and do the impossible.

So choose to believe God today, and...

Something
Good
Is
Going
To
Happen
To
You!

Oral Roberts

About the Author

Educator, evangelist, business man, author, and television personality are among the many titles for which **Oral Roberts** has gained acclaim. He is founder and chancellor of Oral Roberts University, and has been active in ministry for more than forty-eight years. Over that period of time, he has conducted some five hundred evangelistic and healing crusades on six continents and has prayed for over one and one half million sick people through the laying on of hands.

Oral Roberts has also written more than sixty books, including his autobiography, *Expect A Miracle*, and *Miracle of Seed-Faith*, with nearly three million copies in circulation.

Oral Roberts is also founder of University Village, a retirement complex, and the Oral Roberts Evangelistic Association, which sponsors his weekly half-hour television program, *Miracles Now*.

Albury Publishing
P.O. Box 470406
Tulsa, Oklahoma 74147-0406

For information on other books
offered by Albury Publishing, write:

Albury Publishing
P.O. Box 470406
Tulsa, Oklahoma 74147-0406